MEN!

Enjoy!
Margaret G. Bigger

SPORTS

MEN!

Cry Flustered, Frustrated Females Everywhere

by

44 of Those FFFs

Edited by Margaret G. Bigger

Cartoons by Loyd Dillon

aBB

A. Borough Books

44 Flustered, Frustrated Females

A few fellows, too!

Susie Abrams
Bet Ancrum
Margaret Bigger
Susan Blanton
Martha M. Bullen
Anne Burns
Betty Cardo
Marian Carlsson
Elise Carter
Bonnie Chavda
Leeda Currin
Joy Christenbury
Page Courts
Allison Elrod
Judy Gaines
Meredith Galvin
Lish Gennett
Anne Glenn
Lexie Hill
Pam Kelley
Emily Kern
Sandra Krueger

Patty Lazzeri
Nell LaBarge
Ann Ross Liles
Jerry McAlister
Katherine McAdams
Ethel McMillan
Lucinda Miller
Jo Minchew
Vickie Mizak
Bobbie Moore
Harriet Orth
Anne Patterson
Cindy Quayle
Donna Reed
Donna Rymer
Donna Seifert
Katherine Sonner
Faith Summers
Allison Thornton
Deborah Tingle
Linda Wilson
Marjorie Wyatt

Jim Cubbage
Dick Daniels
Loyd Dillon
Alan Elmore
Mike Foreman
John Greig
Albert Kammerle
Hall Miller
Sam Morris
Larry Patterson
Jordan Rich
Keith Shannon
Dave Temple
Ralph Terry
Scott Vallandingham

And thanks to these:
KLIZ - Brainerd, MN
WASH - Washington, DC
WBT - Charlotte, NC
WBZ - Boston, MA
WMAL -Washington, DC
WSLQ - Roanoke, VA
WSOC - Charlotte NC

INTRODUCTION

When Marian Carlsson, a regular contributor to my collections of true anecdotes, related a frustrating incident, she concluded with "MEN!" She suggested that my next book be on that topic. "Women from everywhere will be sending you stories," she predicted.

Yep. Gals of many ages who heard what I was doing said, "I've got one for you!" or "Let me tell you about MINE!"

If you would like to read Marian's stories that started it all, they are the first anecdotes of the Say *WHAT?* and Do *WHAT?* chapters.

If you'd like to add your own tales or lines to my next collection, see the Contributor's Form in the back.

It Starts Really Early!

Meg's friend, who has sons and grandsons, has said for years, "Boys are born making the truck noise." Her husband calls it "the truck gene."

A mother of a girl, Meg didn't believe it until her grandson was born. Yep. First noise! His first word? "Tuk" for truck, which soon became the "F word."

A grandma in Staples, Minnesota, Helen was watching TV, when Dillon, a mere 18 months, grabbed the remote and switched to a football game.

In a hardware store with his mother, Benjamin, 10, disappeared. "Where did he go?" Page wondered aloud.

"Oh, he saw a pretty girl," a clerk said.

Well, not exactly a girl. A gorgeous grown woman —blonde and shapely. As Page spied her, she overheard her son's line, "Look, I've got a new quarter."

It was no surprise, really. She recalled another incident in a grocery store. Benjamin kept smiling, blinking, and following a pretty woman with his eyes. They seemed to move along the same route, so while behind them in line, the stranger remarked, "I must look all right today, 'cause he's given me his stamp of approval."

Benjamin was 10 months old.

"I'm a pacifist. When I had my first son, I was determined that we'd have no guns in our house," said Allison, mother of two boys. "But I've decided that if they don't have them, boys would make them out of toast."

One Sunday morning, as they were headed from the car to the church, she spied Benjamin, 2, with a toy gun. "How did you get that out of the car without my seeing you?" she asked. Just then, they met the minister who was preaching that morning. “Oh, no,” she thought.

But the minister pulled the Good Book from under his arm and made like it was an Uzi. Benjamin jumped behind a bush for the all-out shoot-out. Tyler, her 5-year-old, defended his brother with his finger.

Then along came a 90-year-old man. Allison froze with the thought, “Oh, wow, he’ll be really upset.”

With that, the seasoned citizen cocked his umbrella and “shaca, shaca,” lasered them all dead.

One December Sunday morning, the minister at Martha’s church called the youngsters up to the chancel for “Words with Children.” He asked them what they were hoping to get for Christmas. Several boys and girls called out their choices: “Nintendo!” “Barbie!” “Legos!”

Her son Stuart, 6, spoke up, “I want a Ferrari!”

Say *WHAT?*

Several of Marian's stories have been featured in my books. I was to be interviewed by a radio station in Lexington, Virginia, her hometown, so I notified her that I would be relating her tales. Marian asked someone at the station to let her know when the interview would air.

Upon her return from some errands a few days later, her husband Allan reported that the station had called to say that it would be on in two minutes.

"Well, you listened to it, didn't you?"

"No," said Allan.

Marian was exasperated. "Didn't it occur to you that I might like to know what was said?"

"No, it didn't," he said, looking bewildered.

"MEN!" says she.

Bill kissed his wife Harriet before leaving for work, as he always did. But he didn't return for supper.

"Daddy's not coming home tonight," informed their son Chris. He knew nothing more.

Three nights later, Bill walked in expecting dinner.

"Where have you BEEN?" Harriet demanded to know.

Bill took on an innocent look. "I told you three months ago. You never write anything down."

At the grocery store, an older man was complaining about the price of produce. Mary Anne smiled at the stranger and agreed. They exchanged examples of the cost of similar items in earlier times. "You're too young to know that," he said.

"I'm probably the same age you are," Mary Anne responded smugly, knowing full well that she did not look her age. "I just celebrated my Big 6-0," she added.

"Why you don't look a day over 42!" he said, giving her an up-and-down scrutiny. "A haggard 42."

Kat's friend Jim retired; Nancy, his wife, didn't.

Jim reluctantly agreed to take over the vacuuming.

Later they went shopping, and Jim and Nancy went their separate ways. Then Nancy saw Jim coming across the parking lot pushing a large red self-propelled vacuum cleaner with a headlight and all the attachments in a quiver on the side.

"Why did you buy *that*?" Nancy wanted to know.

Jim grumped, "Because they didn't have a riding one."

Says Lou: "I see no sense in ever making a bed when you're just going to get into it again in 15 hours."

On their first Thanksgiving eve together, Peg was struggling to prepare multiple dishes for the next day. Matt, however, was feeling amorous. "Not tonight," Peg whined, "I've got corn to shuck, beans to string and..."

About 3 a.m., Peg heard kitchen noises. She soon found Matt shucking and grinning. "A deal's a deal!"

CHIC

Just after the road was paved in front of his house, Ed was annoyed that he had to park a block away from home.

When he spotted headlights through his living room window the next night, he was livid! He bolted out the front door, waving his arms at the driver who was, just then, moving the orange cones that had been blocking traffic. "Stop that!" he shouted. "No one drives on that road!" Ed confronted the guy, "Who do you think you are?"

Said his adversary, "I think I'm the guy who paved this road and has returned to test the asphalt."

"I don't care what you've done," Ed persisted with all the testosterone he could muster. "Put back those cones and walk like the rest of us!"

On Bill's first day of retirement, his wife, Nancy, went out shopping. She got home mid-afternoon, and he was waiting for her. "Where have you been?" he asked, furiously tapping his watch. "It's 2:30, and I haven't had lunch yet!"

Architects and other artistic males, says Ethel, are not great spellers. For instance, two weeks after their wedding, they attended an AIA meeting. Her nametag was spelled the way Randy had written it: “Eythel.”

When their daughter was born, they discussed whether to spell Linda with an “i” or a “y.” Before they left the hospital, Randy proudly presented Ethel with a charm bracelet with their new baby’s name on it: “Lyndia.”

As someone who has collected wedding glitch stories for nearly two decades, I had to chuckle over how women’s lib has affected fathers of the bride.

It used to be that all they had to remember to say was “I do” when they handed over their daughters. Now they must say “Her mother and I do.” But it comes out “His mother and I do” or “Her father and I do.” John had his own version: “Wachovia Bank and I do.”

Do *WHAT?*

"My man is intelligent, well-educated (a Ph.D yet!)," says Marian, "but he persists in using the largest carving knife he can find to cut up a banana or peel a peach.

"I point out that the smaller knives nearby would be safer, but he doesn't get the message! MEN!"

Hearing Marian's tale of pointy things like knives and heads, Joy added hers: "Mine takes my good little kitchen knives and uses them outdoors!"

Deborah was telling Anne about her male dog Boo who "aggravates the cat in the daytime and sleeps with her at night."

Anne was nodding. "Just like a husband."

Randy was digging in Ethel's rag bag the other day and got really upset. "That's my shirt!" he said as though he had been deceived.

Like many of his male counterparts, Randy hates to give away clothes. "I might need them some day," he explains.

"He has pants with belt loops too small for today's belts. He gets his junk khakis dry cleaned so they'll last," says his wife. "And remember when ties got narrow? He sent many of his wide ties off to be made narrow. He just couldn't give them up. Now that ties have gotten wide again, those narrow ones are still in the closet."

At an annual Association for Women in Communications awards luncheon, Mary was being honored by her peers and some community movers-and-shakers. One especially prestigious businessman, who could not attend the event, sent a filmed tribute. He concluded with a gesture he apparently assumed would titillate the room full of businesswomen: he stood, swiveled his overweight body and "mooned" them.

Jim, a retired store owner, was being home-schooled. He just couldn't seem to "get the hang" of his computer's intricacies. His family teased that he had to get a social promotion from kindergarten. Nevertheless, his personal tutor was coming more than once a week.

"How many lessons is this is going to take?" wondered his wife Betty to their daughter.

Nancy laughed, "Don't you know that's the only way he has to get that cute girl in his bedroom?"

Boxes of Girl Scout cookies lay abandoned on the rear stairway. Haphazardly, they loomed in crevices and corners on each riser. Clearly a perverse crime had occurred mere inches from Susie's back door.

She cautiously slipped her key into the lock and entered her apartment. Utter silence, except for the clock ticking, calmed her racing heart. However, the view outside the bay window overlooking their deck reinforced her terror—cookies were everywhere!

Holding her breath, Susie entered the bedroom to be greeted by deafening snores. Seemingly, her nude portly prince hadn't budged since she had left to go shopping.

"Honey, wake up!" she implored. "Some sex maniac is stalking Girl Scouts in our complex. Did you hear anything while I was out?"

Groggily, he replied, "Babe, some nut banged on our door and woke me. It must've been a joke, because when I opened up, no one was there."

"Buddy, were you wearing your glasses when you opened the door?"

"Heck no, I couldn't even find my robe."

"Jimmy's mood goes with the sun," his wife Jean attested to a friend in Travelers Rest, South Carolina. "The darker it gets, the nicer he gets."

Just then, Jimmy walked in and patted her on the shoulder.

Jean winked at her friend. "Yep, it's dusk."

"I caught my husband wrestling on the floor with the bride!" said Megan. "It was at my college roommate's wedding, and people were screaming and hollering and it took me awhile to sort it all out."

She explained, "Right before that, the bride had been putting that first piece of cake into the groom's mouth, and all eyes were watching her do that—except my husband's. He saw her short veil catch fire in the flame of the candle on the table. So he jerked the veil. But it didn't come off (what with all the bobby pins in it), so he jerked again, jolting her to the floor. Then he jumped on top of her, banging the flames out with his hands."

Megan sighed, "He was a hero. I just didn't see it that way."

Men hate to have to room with another man on business trips. Larry tells of spending a night with a world-class snorer. He tried the pillow-over-the head, then stuck toilet paper in his ears. The obnoxious roars could not be muffled.

At 2 a.m., he grabbed his pillow and blanket, put them on the floor of the closet, closed the door and fell asleep.

The next morning, his roommate opened the closet door to get his clothes. "Excuse me," he said politely and headed for the bathroom. He left the room quickly without another word.

That made Larry worry. "I could just hear him telling the others, 'You know that guy Larry? He's a real weirdo!'"

"...and his tools are all over the bedroom," Katherine complained to her mother-in-law, hoping for some sympathy —or advice—on managing her new husband.

The older woman smiled with understanding. "Do you know what is worse than a dirty boy's room?"

Katherine shook her head.

"It's a clean boy's room, because that means the boy isn't living there."

Driving Directionless

"I don't know about other men, but my Kemp definitely has an attitude—a driving attitude," says Lexie.

When Kemp hits the road, his attitude is "Make way! Clear the path, here I come, ready or not!" In his mind, according to Lexie, there's a conspiracy out there and in every car is a driver with an insidious plan to keep him from reaching his destination.

Their only conversation is his one-sided barrage toward the drivers behind, in front of, or on the side of his car. To those behind: "Get off my bumper, man! You've been riding it for miles. You want the whole road?" or "You in a hurry?" In line, waiting for the light to change, the cars ahead never move fast enough. "So what's the matter? Waiting for the spirit to move you?"

Lane-switchers really stir his wrath, but he is the champion lane-changer. He can maneuver into a space for a

Volkswagen. For those who pull in front, he mutters, "You stupid idiot, didn't anybody teach you how to drive? Now that you're here, MOVE ON!" Anytime he's waiting behind someone trying to turn, he seems to think the driver and the car should just evaporate so he can go.

"To take an out-of-town trip with Kemp requires all the patience I can muster," says Lexie. "Forget the agreed upon time for departure; he has ants in his pants 30 minutes ahead of time and is raring to go."

Once they're on the way, his course is set. He won't look back, let up, slow down or stop until he reaches the destination. The distance they travel is limited to how long he can last without going to the bathroom.

Lexie will beg, plead, appeal to his compassion to stop for food or to stretch their legs.

Finally, he will say, "Look for the Hardee's sign in the next town, and we'll stop."

Lexie will point to the sign in the distance on the right. Then she will comb her hair and gather her purse, relieved to be getting out of the car when... ZOOM right on by.

Dumbfounded she'll say, "That was Hardee's."

He'll frown. "But you didn't tell me in time to stop."

Pam, a reporter from *The Charlotte Observer*, tells of riding with her husband on Interstate 64, somewhere in West Virginia. She was dozing while he was driving, when she felt the car veer left, then right. Pam jerked awake and braced for disaster. There sat hubby with a road atlas spread across his lap.

"You need help?" she asked.

"No. I'm just looking," said Trent.

Pam later considered that remark. "Just looking. We are driving 70 miles per hour, we are in no way lost, but he is just perusing the map of West Virginia. For pleasure."

On a trip from Fort Worth, Texas to Alberta, Canada, Jeff and Faith were cruising along Interstate 70 approaching Denver. Jeff noticed a road sign "Boulder 35 miles."

"Great!" he said excitedly. "We'll stop and see Boulder Dam."

"Boulder Dam? That's not in Colorado," said Faith.

Jeff replied with a definite, "Yes, it *is*!"

Later, as they approached a toll gate, Jeff eagerly asked, "How many more miles to Boulder Dam?"

With a smug grin, the tollgate keeper replied, "Eight hundred ninety-seven miles that way," pointing west.

My bridge group was discussing the male reluctance—or refusal—to ask directions.

I had just noted, "My husband used to have a great sense of direction. Not anymore, but he STILL won't ask for directions."

"Of course not!" said Jerry, "That's why Moses roamed the desert for 40 years."

"Why do you think the male symbol goes around in a circle before it points northeast?" someone added.

How come...?

His second favorite after-dark exercise is surfing (TV channels or the net)?

A male fan will go into debt to buy a PSL for his favorite sport, but balks at spending money to beautify his home?

He endures rain, sleet, wind or snow for a football game but finds it too uncomfortable to sit through a ballet recital?

A man can remember sports statistics from 20 years ago, but can live with a woman for two decades and have no idea what kind of jewelry, flowers or perfume she prefers?

He can listen to the self-help tapes you gave him and still not change a single thing?

He'll ask, "Is that a new dress?" of one you've had for 20 years, but will never notice the one you bought just last week?

He collects a variety of tools, but can't seem to find the right one when you want something done?

Although mesmerized by the weather channel, he's rarely outdoors on weekdays except to get to and from his car?

Guys who act macho usually aren't?

How come...?

Retired husbands soon acquire an attribute of the Almighty—omnipresence?

When he finally agrees to stop and ask directions, he will invariably approach someone who looks like the village idiot or another male who is as lost as he is?

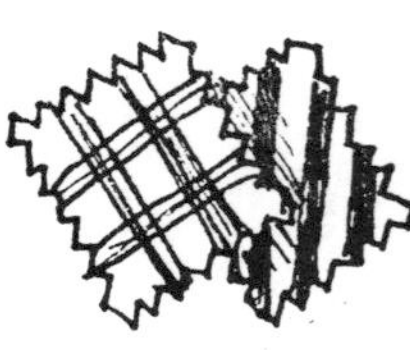

Even the guys who are not colorblind can't seem to match a jacket, pants, tie and shirt?

He's very particular about the mattress he sleeps on during the week, but his favorite weekends are the ones when he sleeps on the ground with the bugs?

He can spend three hours in a sports bar but is ready to leave a wedding reception in 30 minutes?

An expectant father who adamantly wants a boy will get himself firmly wrapped around his daughter's little finger, a lifetime condition?

He knows exactly what you're doing wrong until he tries it himself?

An adult male is incapable of replacing a roll of toilet tissue?

He can't find anything in the refrigerator but the beer?

And how come...?

Males are the ones most likely to peruse a Victoria's Secret catalog but are least likely to buy anything out of it?

When women have a mid-life crisis, we go for a facelift; when men have a mid-life crisis, they go for someone else's new face?

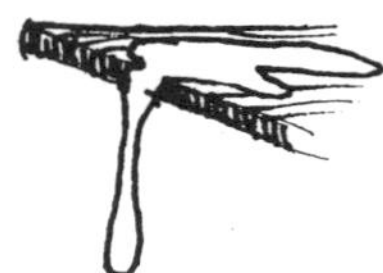

Your husband obsesses over microscopic spots on his necktie yet never sees the half-carton of milk dripping off the kitchen table?

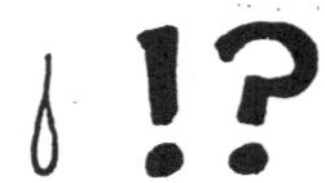

A fellow can explain complicated procedures to his peers but can't tell his wife what he did on his last business trip?

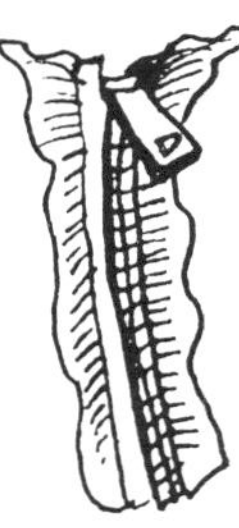

The same guy who was disappointed when no one commented about his tiny-snowmen tie July 4th, insists that nobody will notice the unstitched placket that makes his fly protrude?

He can fold a large map back into its original form but can't fold a towel out of the dryer?

Cigars have become so popular since the Clinton scandal?

A man is the king of his castle, but his wife is the maid?

You can't change a man unless he's still wearing diapers?

Competing with sex, sports stay on the brain.

A first-time dad, Frank made sure that Zack watched the Dolphins game with him his first weekend home from the maternity hospital. Frank wanted to make sure his son understood what it is to be male.

So how come Mike took his 2-year-old squirrel hunting anyway? This Virginia dad was supposed to be baby-sitting. Guess this was his idea of "killing two birds with one stone."

No doubt, he'll never do that again. He was holding little Michael in one arm and tried shooting with the other hand. Kaboom! Michael wet him.

"My husband knows the scores of 17 Super Bowls," says Emily, "but can't remember his siblings' birthdays."

"You're a real golfer," said Frank proudly, "when you're driving past a golf course and see a guy at the tee and you stop so you won't disturb his swing."

Allison had selected the colors to remodel the kitchen of their Atlanta home: white cabinets, black counter tops and sunny yellow walls.

Steve, a University of Georgia grad, was incensed. "Allison, I will *not have* a Georgia Tech kitchen!"

After catching Emily weeping over a Lassie re-run she was watching with the kids, Mark teased her most of the week-end for being so sentimental over a silly animal show.

Then Emily walked into the family room during a Monday Night Football commercial break and noticed some silly animals on the screen croaking about beer. As she started to speak, Mark held up his hand for her to wait. Together, they watched the poignant ending to the large beer-loving frog

commercial. Emily laughed until she noticed his serious look.
"Now that's great television," he sighed.

Much to the dismay of the mother of the bride, all of the ushers wore Sony Walkman earphones during the ceremony.

The nerve of that bride! She'd scheduled her Birmingham wedding during the Auburn-Alabama football game!

A Carolina graduate, the groom didn't know his team would get invited to the Gator Bowl on his wedding day.

Not one of the couple's contemporaries came!

Until recent years, this never would have happened:

"My husband kept stopping along the way to buy football magazines, in case he ran out of things to do on the honeymoon," related Patty, a Massachusetts bride.

"Six stores to get six magazines."

But this happened in the '60s, when a honeymoon's first night was a major event:

While preparing to make her grand entrance in her new peignoir set, Anne dropped her diamond down the drain in the hotel bathroom. A plumber came promptly. He and her groom immediately discovered a mutual bond. Both were Clemson graduates. And so, for the next two hours, they drank and talked Clemson football, while the bride sat barefoot in her slip and her husband's jacket, silently stewing.

At 4 a.m., she made her belated—and futile—entrance. "We were too tired," she said. On reflection, Anne added, "If that plumber had been from any other school, he would've been out of there."

Jim's uncle's friend, who was in the real estate business, offered him and his bride a free chalet for their honeymoon.

No wonder it was free—it was empty! No bed. No other furniture. No kitchen equipment. Only a TV. They poured champagne into borrowed glasses, sliced some cheese with a pocket knife and hung a towel over the window.

To Jim, It was not a total loss. They could lie on the floor and watch the Super Bowl.

This one beats all!

The bride was telling her own story on a radio talk show in North Carolina. It went something like this:

"My husband's a racing fanatic, so we spent our first night at the Rockingham Motor Speedway...in the infield...in a tent...in rain and sleet...with his cousin. The storm was so bad that the tent collapsed, and we had to spend the rest of the night in the car."

"The cousin, too?"

"Yes, but the rest of the time, we stayed in a motel."

"The cousin, too?"

"Uh huh. He slept in one bed, and we were in the other. I keep telling my husband that we need another honeymoon."

"Another?" the host hooted. "Lady, you never had one!"

Betcha…!

If a man ever entered a dark bathroom and sat down on cold, wet porcelain, he would become more considerate about putting down the toilet seat!

If he had to concentrate on his job and be both slave and nurturer to his spouse and children while suffering with PMS, he'd be grouchy, too.

Had men traditionally been the primary homemakers, home appliances would have been invented long before they were.

If males were the ones to get pregnant, we'd have no worries about population explosion.

BABY

Have you heard?
Males have selective hearing.

Our little daughter, Joy, stood at the footstool in our den, looking at her favorite picture book. She touched her finger to the cat on the cover and said, "Kit-ty."

"Did you hear that? Did you hear that?" my husband exclaimed, jumping up from his chair. "She said 'Daddy'!"

"My husband keeps the television volume low," says Ethel, "but when I speak above it, he claims he doesn't hear me."

"Mine hears fine when we're having a discussion," attests Annie. "It's when I ask him to do something around the house that he becomes deaf."

From the days of Archie Bunker, who called a gynecologist a "groincologyst," Donna has laughingly noted how men can reinvent the English language. Her father-in-law, for instance, recounted a scuba diving experience, saying there were "gropers" in the ocean.

"I believe groupers were the creatures in mind," said this woman from Winfield, Illinois.

Later, her husband Ernie made an appointment for an MRI scan. He reported that the nurse had asked him if he could relax with music during the procedure or, if he might be claustrophobic and need to be "seduced."

Donna raised an eyebrow. "I *assume* she asked if he needed to be sedated."

When asked a question, Linda's son John will sometimes say "Huh?" He's not hard of hearing, and he knows what was asked. He finally admitted that it gives him a moment to decide what *she* wants to hear.

Have you noticed?
Men rarely notice.

While Richard and Anne were on a business trip to Toronto, Anne went to a beauty salon near the convention center. Amazed by the prices, she got a shampoo and set with no extras.

As she was walking out, Richard, who had been waiting for her, exclaimed, "What did that woman do to make your hair turn gray?!"

Anne shook her head gently. "It wasn't what she did. It's what she *didn't* do."

Richard's eyes went out of focus. He never knew that Anne had been coloring her hair for ten years.

Preparing to go out, Cindy turned to her husband, "Do I look all right?"

"Yes."

Later, they were in a department store, where they had shopped for quite awhile. The Zephyr Hills, Florida mom tried to put her hands in her pocket. What was wrong? Her maternity shorts were wrong side out – pockets hanging, seams showing, elastic front flapping.

Cindy was mortified. "Why did you say I looked okay?"

Hubby was sheepish. "I didn't look at you."

Most of my life, I have worn my hair long. Not back-tickling, but certainly shoulder-brushing. In a quest for change, newness, lightheartedness, I let my beautician cut it all the way up to my ears. I hardly recognized myself. Our teenage daughter and I could hardly wait for Randy to come home to hear his reaction.

He never mentioned the change! That night, Joy and I agreed not to bring up the subject and see how long it took him to notice. Every day, when she came home from school, she'd ask, "Has he noticed yet?" I'd just shake my head.

A month later, at his law firm's picnic, one of several

women nearby asked, "How do you like your wife's hair?"

He glanced at me and said, "Well, my mother taught me that, if you can't say something nice, don't say anything at all."

While dating, Marjorie made the colossal mistake of asking Jeff what he thought she weighed. She was offended when he said, "About 160." Twenty pounds high!

Her feelings were hurt again when she told her actual weight. "What?" he said. "I guessed *low!*"

At 30, Bee's hair began turning prematurely gray; by 40, it was nearly white. She turned to her hairdresser for help.

Some time later, her father-in-law came to visit from Florida. "Bee!" he said. "The last time I saw you, you had gray hair!"

Bee was smiling, as her husband Shep turned to look at her. "Oh, yes," he said thoughtfully, "you did."

Masculine Misinterpretations

Wise use of money - buying a big boat or luxury car.
Foolish use of money - purchasing nice bedroom furniture that "no one will see."

Old - a car after one year.
New (or like new) - a favorite plaid sport coat, at least 20 years old.

Really talking - saying "Yep" and "Nope," even making occasional eye contact, when a commercial interrupts a ball game.
Really listening - something done while reading the newspaper, clicking the TV remote or speeding in the car.

Washing the car - soaping, rinsing, drying, waxing, buffing, polishing, vacuuming, detailing the tires, shining the chrome.

Washing dishes - piling plates, mugs, etc. in the sink and turning on the cold water.

Hide - deliberately put out of his reach, as in "Where did you hide my pipe?"

Find - a macho toy at a bargain, as in "That's a real find!"

Great date - one that ends with sex—or one that begins with sex—or one that skips everything else.

Great mate - one who will cater to your ego, stomach and sexual desires at no charge. (If this person exists, better keep it a secret.)

Foreplay - a quick compliment and then "that look."

Feelings - physical ailments, never emotions.

Wedding band - a device designed to cut off circulation. (It better, buddy!)

Wrestling match - what guys watch on TV and do in bed.

Grocery store - where you pick up a six-pack and a date.

Necktie - (if you're young) idiotic useless piece of garbage, (if you're middle-age) great way to express yourself, or (if you're old) a bib.

Garage - place to keep tools, wood, beer, assorted junk and used male toys, adjacent to the driveway, where cars are parked. (In emergencies: great place to hide from HER.)

Couch - personal ball game seat during sports seasons; personal bed, preferably on Sundays.

What's so distasteful about shopping?

"My husband won't buy anything unless I'm with him," says Ethel, "but he won't buy shoes unless they are 'his size.' He has gained weight, but he must have 'his size' which means that he rejects most of the ones he tries on."

She reports that he must have 25 pairs in his closet (from the last 30 years), which don't fit.

If he allows his "significant other" to buy his clothes (which most men do), then with the exception of shoes, sports equipment and male toys, the only things he is expected to purchase are gifts for that special person. Even that must go against his nature.

During the holidays, Shep saw a negligee in a department store window that he thought would please his wife, Bee.

A dentist, he sent his nurse in to buy it. He was truly happy with himself, for this year, instead of asking what she wanted, he would have a wonderful surprise.

Shep was beaming when Bee opened his gift in front of the rest of the family. “I thought it looked like you,” he told her.

The others burst out laughing. Bee pulled out of the box a negligee identical to the old one she was wearing.

“What would you like for Christmas?” Dick asked.

“I think I’d like a ring,” said Ann Ross, his wife.

Dick looked surprised. “But you already have one.”

An NFL player admitted that he, too, waits until the last minute to Christmas shop. Why?

“Because in five minutes, I get a headache from looking at the prices,” he said.

Hmmm. With all those NFL megabucks?

MERRY CHRISTMAS, HONEY

Carter could not get over Mary's disappointment with his Christmas gift. "They were very expensive!" he told his daughter. "And she really needed them."

"I know Daddy," she said, "But it's not very romantic to give your wife a set of tires."

They were both on a diet, so David gave Pam a heart of lettuce wrapped in red paper for Valentine.

She served it for supper.

"Did Andrew send you flowers for Valentine?" her college roommate asked.

Maggie didn't answer. Her boyfriend, who was at Princeton, hadn't even sent her a card. Other friends (who happened to be male) had given her candy.

Finally, on Valentine's Day, she saw an envelope from him in her post office box. It was a letter! At the end was a terse verse: "Woses are wed. Violets are blue. Thugar ith thweet. Oo bulls go moo?"

She screamed with rage, frustration and hurt. Her roommates and friends on her hall gathered to read the crazy words and commiserate.

When she returned from the library that night, a paper banner stretched across the room above Maggie's bed. It read: "Oo bulls go moo?"

The next February, Andrew sent her a card for Groundhog's Day *and* Valentine.

"What did Randy give you?" my friends would ask.

Although we never went steady (possibly because we went to colleges hundreds of miles apart and then he served in the Navy), Randy and I dated for seven years.

It was embarrassing every Christmas, birthday or whatever to have to squeak a meek, "Uh, nothing."

Other guys whom I had dated only a few times would send flowers or bring perfume. We got engaged anyway the Thanksgiving of my senior year and his last year in the Navy.

For Christmas, he gave me a gold watch. I was overwhelmed.

"Why didn't you ever give me anything all those other Christmases?" I asked when I had finished gushing over the wonderful watch.

He shrugged. "My mother told me never to give a gift to a girl unless I was serious."

My husband definitely has the men-hate-to-shop syndrome. Certainly, he was showing true love the first Christmas of our married life, when he bought me a romantically elegant nightgown and matching wispy robe.

Apparently, he was so ill-at-ease among the lingerie in a department store, that he waited 'til just before closing time to rush in.

Because I worked for the radio station across the street, the clerk recognized our last name when Randy handed her his charge card. Later, she told me what happened.

He pointed to a mannequin and said, "I want one of those! And a box." He was looking around, probably hoping no one would notice him there.

As soon as Randy had the package in hand, he ran down the indoor fire escape, pushed open the door to the street—and set off the alarm, bringing salespeople from every corner.

From my man with the shopping aversion came a surprise gift one afternoon: a king-sized fitted sheet with two king-sized pillowcases. They had enormous flowers, each larger than my head which had "big hair" at the time. They were purple, orange, yellow and two shades of pink. In spaces between the blossoms were polka dots on a bright green field. Our bedroom walls had the look of elegant red damask; the furniture, mahogany antiques; the bed, a double four-poster.

"Thank you Sweetheart," I said, trying to be gracious. "But why did you buy these?"

"They were on sale," he said matter-of-factly.

"But we don't have a king-sized bed."

"We will someday," he said.

Seven years later, we got the bed to go with the sheet.

"Do you have a dog?" a new acquaintance asked Lucinda, who is married to Hall.

"Yes," she said. "Digory is the birthday present I got instead of kitchen cabinets."

Asked what she wanted for her birthday, Anne Marie didn't have a suggestion at first.

"Would you like a ceiling fan?" hubby questioned.

"Yes," she said sarcastically, "that's what I really want for my 26th birthday."

The very next day she turned 26, and when Anne Marie walked into the kitchen, there was a huge box on the counter: her new ceiling fan. But on top of that box was a smaller one.

"Oh, he did think of something special and personal for me," she thought warmly, while opening the package.

Surprise! It was a wooden toilet lid.

Oh, those do-it-yourselfers!

"I hate it when Jeff says, 'It'll only take me half a day,'" confided Marjorie from Birmingham.

"The first time, he was putting in a bathtub. We were without water three days. The second, installing a water heater: four days! I had to run across the street to a friend's house every time I needed to go to the bathroom. He didn't."

Alvin was going to show son Ryan how to do a brake job. Up went the rusty teenage hand-me-down Chevy onto the jack. They fiddled and faddled most of a Saturday. No luck. Ooops! In the process, Alvin broke the emergency brake.

Always seeking to avoid paying professionals, Frank chose a breezy fall day to paint the ceiling of his new self-constructed carport. In an effort to prevent spilling the white oil-based paint, he draped his ladder with a canvas, which covered an area of the floor as well. Atop the ladder, he placed a nearly full gallon of paint.

Nature called. And the wind blew. The canvas became a sail, fluttering with each gust, moving the ladder boat-like and spilling the paint. By the time Frank had returned, the wind had painted the carport FLOOR. Done free!

"My husband has never met a repair project that couldn't be conquered by a roll of duct tape," declares Emily.

Having no need for clumsy wrenches or screwdrivers, Mark's recent "repairs" include taping part of the swing set together, strapping the seat onto the kids' tractor and sticking the broken shelf on the refrigerator door back in place.

"Unfortunately," says Emily, "we'll never be able to move one of the salad dressing bottles from its current position. Ever."

Mark has used the gummy gray matter to tape a torn

grill cover, fix holes in the kiddie pool and revive essential items like a broken shampoo bottle. He and other guys exchange usage ideas. His friend John proudly tells of a ski trip saved by duct tape. Rather than search for a needle and thread, John taped a large rip in his ski pants and claimed they were even warmer than before.

Emily shook her head. "That's male bonding, I guess."

The kitchen of their rented apartment in historic Wilmington, North Carolina was an awful orangy-red. Before repainting, Bert put on a mask and used the power sander. Red dust went everywhere. Bert kept sanding. More red dust. "You'd think he'd stop!" recalled Katherine. "Despite the mask, he blew red stuff from his nose for a week!"

Not all men are alike.

"Mark's mechanically challenged," says his wife Emily. "When a light bulb burns out, he moves to another room."

Are they downright helpless — or suspiciously smart?

"My husband has never learned to load the dishwasher properly," said Margie. "I prefer doing it myself, so the china and glasses won't be chipped."

She thought a moment, grinning. "But then I just never could figure out how to pull that little handle on the lawn mower hard enough to make it start."

Like most men, Randy is a baby when he's sick, expecting all the mothering he got back then.

"If you have three children," says Ethel, his wife, who has three children, "suddenly you have four!"

She thought a moment. "But if *you're* sick, he heads to the office and calls out, 'See you at lunch!' That means I'm supposed to have it ready for him."

“Men are wonderful, but you have to tell them what to do and how to do it,” Jennifer confided to Lish, her mother. “Like, if the baby’s crying, you have to say, ‘put a pacifier in her mouth.’”

Home with the early stages of the flu, Mark made consistent use of the bell Emily had placed near his bed. He rang for the thermometer just out of reach, for help with his pillows, to bring the medicine, to open the medicine bottle, to get some water and straighten his blankets. He communicated through groans and sighs, clearly too sick to move.

Later, Emily tiptoed upstairs with a pot of lemon tea and some toast. To her surprise, Mark was sitting straight up in bed intently watching the sports channel. The remote had magically moved from the top of the TV to his hand.

Thinking fast, he moaned, “Um, I just needed to see one last game before I lapsed into a coma.” He coughed and grinned sheepishly. “Got any pretzels?”

Male Malady: Kitchen Blindness

This syndrome primarily affecting men won't be found in any medical literature, as many doctors are unaware that they have it themselves. Here are the most common symptoms, according to Marian:

* **The inability to see anything spilled.**

A man who can spot a speck of dirt on a newly washed car from 200 feet away will not notice the thick dark goo oozing off the kitchen counter onto the floor unless he steps in it, and then only if he's barefoot. Maybe.

* **The inability to clean up a mess.**

The same guy who spends hours buffing his car with a chamois has the idea that cleaning up kitchen spills involves merely waving a small piece of dry paper towel in the general direction of the mess. Try that on your car, buddy, the next time a bird baptizes it!

* **The inability to find something.**

If you can't leave what you're stirring on the stove and ask him to hand you the garlic press, he'll ask, "Where is it?"

And you'll reply, "In the same place it's been for the last 10 years, the top drawer to the right of the sink."

He'll open the drawer an inch and announce triumphantly, "It's not there!" Even if he can be persuaded to open the drawer all the way, he still won't see it unless a tag is attached proclaiming in bright red letters, GARLIC PRESS. Maybe.

* **The inability to observe things out-of-place.**

You confront him with the partially melted remains of the plastic cover of your recipe book and ask, "How could you not see that this was on top of the toaster oven when you turned it on?"

He'll shrug and say, "I dunno," looking not at all guilty, just helpless.

Proven Remedy:

Since there is no cure for this malady short of divorce, the best remedy, says Marian, is to "get into that shiny, spot-free car and head for the nearest restaurant and let them worry about cleaning up."

What Price Friendship?

Why is it that men do terrible things to a friend who is getting married? Jealousy? Join-the-confinement-club initiation? Gotcha back? Bachelor parties (particularly in the South) are notorious for terrible pranks.

Women don't do such things at bachelorette parties.

Think about it: these people, usually the ones chosen for the wedding party, are supposed to be his closest friends.

If a bride's friends shaved her head the night before her wedding, they could forget the friendship. She'd probably have them arrested for assault!

And what do you think she'd do if they:

Painted her body from head to toe with India ink, which does not wash off? (It has to wear off.)

Tied her to a tree in the woods or chained her to a toilet at home?

Stripped her of everything but boots and rode her around town in the back of a pickup truck?

Got her arrested (for drunkenness, indecent exposure, whatever) so she would spend the night before her wedding in jail?

Took off her underwear, cut it in little pieces and carried them as hankies during the wedding ceremony?

Put her in a room alone with a male stripper, a stranger!?

Got her drunk, took all her money, IDs and credit cards and put her on transportation out of town?

In one of the latter scenarios, the bride got a call from Nome, Alaska. The groom's Navy buddies had put him on a freight plane from Charleston, South Carolina. Fortunately, the bachelor party was on a Wednesday, so he made it to the Saturday wedding in Richmond, Virginia.

But in another case, the so-called friends put the drunk groom on a commercial flight from South Carolina to California. There was time for him to get back, but they didn't count on the airport getting "socked in" by fog. He didn't make it in time. The bride sued him for the cost of the wedding and refused to marry him.

Did he keep those same friends?

Probably.

Tying the (marriage) knot that binds.

It's what many males fear the most: to be "tied down." And yet, statistics show that married men are more content and live longer. If his wife dies or if there is a divorce, what is the first thing a man does? Look for another woman, of course.

The subject was weddings. "I'm just leasing," the young man from Atlanta reported defiantly.

"But his option to buy has almost run out," retorted his woman.

"I do," said a Hickory, North Carolina groom. He spun from his place, plucked out a $50 bill, strode to an usher and handed it to him. It was the pay-off of a longstanding bet that he'd never say those two words.

Mike, the Winchester, Virginia clerk of court recalls issuing a marriage license to a town character and his eighth bride. Mike asked about the other wives.

"All of them are dead but one," said the groom.

"Just think," said Mike, "When you die and go to Heaven, they'll all be waiting for you."

"Yeah, it makes me want to go to the other place."

Mike had always heard that he had traded his first wife for a Model T Ford and questioned, "Is it true?"

"Yes," the oldster said. "And I want to tell you something. The car wasn't a damn bit better than she was."

When asked whether he took his bride as his wife, the Rice University football player reached into his pocket for a quarter. He held it up for his minister and the congregation to see. "Heads!" he called.

The burly guy flipped it high, slapped it on the back of his hand and slowly peeked at the results. "I do!"

Why is it that a groom gets so nervous during the wedding ceremony? Could it be that he knows those 20 minutes will change his life forever?

The groom sank downward, out cold.

His best man and an usher caught him. Stood him back up. Braced him. Even nodded his head, when he should have said, "I do."

A few years later, the couple got an annulment. The groom claimed he "didn't know what he was doing."

As he faced his bride to repeat the vows, the groom broke down. No words, only tears came out.

Five minutes of crying was too long, especially for his old man. Both father and son were military men, and everyone knows that this breed doesn't show emotion.

The groom's father stood it as long as he could. Then he strode to the front. "Suck it up son," he ordered.

Son sucked.

Told that he could kiss his bride, a Knoxville, Tennessee groom grimaced, "Do I have to?"

His bride had thrown up just before the ceremony.

When a New Jersey priest said, "You may now kiss Mrs. Metzer," the groom spun, stepped a pew away and planted one on his mother.

We've all heard of a groom who got "cold feet" and "couldn't go through with it."

However, the most inconsiderate was surely the one in Pennsylvania who ran away with the gifts.

A Georgia bride got tickled. So did her groom. And his bladder didn't hold.

You gotta love a guy who tries to be a good dad.

While working at his computer, Scott agreed to hold his infant Nicole, while Mom was busy. His home office was hot, and he began to sweat. In fact, the entire front of this shirt was wet.

Oh, oh, maybe Nicole's diaper was leaking.

Oh, oh, he hadn't noticed. No diaper!

Susan tells of the changes (pun intended) in their house after she and Joe brought their triplets home from the hospital.

A few weeks into the routine, Joe offered to do night duty and slept on the floor of the babies' room.

"He was afraid he wouldn't hear them," Susan laughed. "Three babies, and he didn't think he'd hear them!"

Just a few nights after their baby came home, Roy and his wife, Bobbie, switched roles for the wee-hours feeding. Roy gallantly offered to let her sleep.

But Bobbie couldn't sleep, waiting for him to return to bed. Concerned, she got up to check on him. There he was, groggily warming a Pepsi bottle.

Ralph had just finished scolding Hannah for putting hot coffee into a plastic cup. He had explained why: the cup would melt.

Then he inadvertently placed the filled cup on the stove's burner. Lesson learned.

Eating her salad before dinner, Jordan's daughter Lindsey was a bit messy. Jordan picked up a piece of cauliflower from the table and popped it into his mouth. It tasted weird.

Lindsey watched him curiously. "Dad, why are you eating my Pla-Doh?"

Dick from Roanoke, Virginia confessed a "huge error" he'd made with his young son, John William, who was getting used to drinking from a cup with no top. He liked the "twirly-curly" straw but could be a little messy.

Dick had shown him how to suck up his spills with the cute straw. That, of course, was much more fun than drinking from the cup, so John William would deliberately pour out his milk and "schluurp!"

Thomas stopped by a friend's home briefly and spoke with his friend's mother, Elise. "I'm in a hurry," said Thomas. "Tommy's in the car."

"You should never leave a child alone in a car," cautioned Elise.

"Oh, he's all right. Look," said Thomas turning toward the old Chrysler with the push-button gears.

They looked—and watched the car roll down a hill and crash into a tree.

The only injury: Daddy's pride.

Keith admits he's not much of a cook. His older daughter Kathleen confirms it. As a first grader, she announced that her favorite food was Tuna Helper.

One night when Keith had to teach a college class, he left dinner with the sitter. Later, he called Kathleen and asked, "Did you have a good supper?"

"No," said Kathleen. "We ate what you fixed."

Jean, a mother from Baltimore, had to be at church early on Easter Sunday, so she asked her husband Mike to help the girls dress and bring them in time for the children's parade. Libby, 5, and Kitty, 3, were both in the procession.

And so, during the service, Mom turned around to see her girls proudly parading down the aisle in their pretty new slips.

Sensible Solutions to Silly Dilemmas (or Gals Fight Back)

Somewhere around 50, the men in our lives begin making strange noises. It's as though they have swallowed a horn mouthpiece and snuffed up an amplifier. The amazing thing about all this is that they're totally oblivious to their own cacophony. They sleep through it all.

Until a couples party, I thought I was the only wakeful wife. Every woman there was describing my same plight from her point of view.

"The snoring's not so bad," commented one. "It's the snorting that really gets to me."

"Yeah," said another, "makes your adrenalin run. And there you are stiff, jolted sleepless. And there he is, sleeping like a baby."

A knowing nod. "And it takes at least an hour for the adrenalin to absorb, so what do you do?"

"I turn on the light and read," said a novice.

"Well, I take sleeping pills," said another.

We didn't see that as even a short-term response. "Bad habit." "You could get addicted."

A seasoned veteran of this phenomenon sighed. "Sometimes I get up and do housework."

"I used to have that problem," said Anne, the only calm person in the discussion. "But I bought earplugs."

Another friend admitted spending half her nights in a spare bedroom. Probably the most opinionated of the group reacted with anger. "*He's* the one making the noise, why should *I* be the one to leave?"

Had anyone visited a "sleep clinic" ? Nope. Would they badger their husbands to go? Nope. A futile exercise. All our men are in denial.

We all knew of another couple in their late 50s who were buying a new house—not down-sizing, but getting "his" and "her" bedrooms.

"You know that sleeping porch we're adding for the grandchildren?" Most of us had heard about their building project. "Well, that's for Stan."

Men usually tilt a pre-nuptial agreement in their favor in proportion to their wealth. Right?

When Margaret's intended insisted on a "pre-nupt," she did some negotiating in her own favor. It's in the contract: he must take her out to dinner every night.

"Didn't I see Rod driving a new Miata?" a friend asked.

"He just drove it into the driveway one night," said Holly in a peeved tone. Then she smiled. "So I went out and got a passport so I can take that trip to Germany I've wanted."

To Hall, leaves were "extended ground cover," an excuse not to mow. Then he got a pup who liked to play in them. Lucinda, Hall's wife, suddenly got smart. She sprinkled dog food around the barely buried cable that carried ESPN into the house. "I now have leaves bagged that will keep recycling busy for a year and azaleas to die for, " says Lucinda. "If only the cable went through the den."

It's a "GIVEN" that guys...

Assume a football game is more important than a close relative's funeral. (If the deceased were a male, he would understand.)

In the '50s, saw nothing wrong with an all-male city club with a women's entrance on the side or rear of the building.

Still see nothing wrong with a country club with prime tee times set aside for males.

Think it's funny when other guys burp or pass gas but disgusting when a girlfriend or wife does it.

Dread power outages mainly because they'll miss their favorite TV shows and sports channels.

Have an "I can do it myself, Mommy" mind-set, which lasts throughout male adulthood, with disastrous results—as in plumbing and electrical mishaps.

Don't "do" lunch; YOU'RE supposed to fix it.

Expect their wives to provide a heart-healthy diet but go out and order steak, fries and beer.

Set the thermostat lower on any night they can't already see their breath.

It's a "GIVEN" that guys...

Pick their noses at stoplights.

Will claim the house doesn't need vacuuming if they think they might have to help.

At some time in their lives, must own a pickup truck, a motorcycle or (the ultimate) a Humvee.

Don't "get it" when their significant other wants to stop at cuddling.

Want to skip the details and get to the basics on every topic, especially sex.

Even those who never read a book or a newspaper will diligently study *Sports Illustrated's* swimsuit issue.

Would rather go (select one: hunting, fishing, hiking, boating, golfing, eat liver, do ANYTHING) than shop.

Can't seem to understand the meaning of "no."

Spell the word "relationship" with three letters.

Never have headaches at bedtime.

Despite all our complaints, are truly loveable!

BEER
BEER
SIX BOTTLES

What *really* makes a man happy:

Sex and a six-pack.

A hot video and a cold beer.

A bad foreign film and a good domestic ale.

A great German sausage, sauerkraut and a stein of lager.

A TV remote in one hand and a can of Bud in the other.

A day at the races and a night at a bar.

A mildly alcoholic drink made from malt, hops, etc.

Sex and a six-pack.

Disclaimer *

Lest anyone think disparagingly about my husband, I want to set the record straight.

Randy is the most thoughtful, kind, loving, compassionate man I know. A born peacemaker, he has raised his voice only twice in my presence—when our teenager pushed all his buttons at once. Sports are the games he plays with our grandson—or the ones he watches when convenient.

The worst comment he ever makes about my cooking is that it's "nourishing," and he actually shares the TV remote!

Lest anyone think he's abnormal, I must admit that there are still times when our daughter Joy and I look at each other, roll our eyes and huff, "MEN!"

* Randy says this word should be "Atonement" as in appease, apology, self-reproach, reparation and do penance (such as sackcloth and ashes and self-flagellation).

MEN!

Other Humor Titles by A. Borough Books

If you enjoyed this book, you're sure to like:

You've GOT to Have a Sense of Humor to Have a Wedding

Humorous, outrageous & disastrous true tales from the engagement through the honeymoon + advice not found in wedding guides.

Margaret G. Bigger Cartoons by Loyd Dillon Paperback
Standard print - 1997, Third Printing April 1998 pp. 128 $9.95

MotherHoot - The Lighter Side of Motherhood

True anecdotes about moms from pregnancy through grandmotherhood

Margaret G. Bigger Cartoons by Loyd Dillon Paperback
Standard print - 1999, Second Printing June 1999 pp. 128 $9.95

Kitties & All That Litter -

Mewsings, GRRRoaners, true cat tales and kitty limericks by 26 cat-loving curmudgeons.

Edited/Curtailed by Margaret G. Bigger Cat-tooned by Loyd Dillon Paperback
LARGE PRINT-1999 pp. 96 $7.50

Gray-Haired Grins & Giggles

Guess What! Grammy & Grandy have a sense of humor, too!
True tales from childhood to retirement by 45 senior authors

Edited by Margaret G. Bigger Cartoons by Loyd Dillon Paperback
Standard print - 1995, Fourth Printing June 1996 pp. 128 $12.95
LARGE PRINT - 1998, somewhat abridged pp. 140 $13.95

Also by Margaret Bigger & Loyd Dillon:

Recalling Your Memories on Paper, Tape or Videotape Self-help guide to preserving memoirs & photos for your family - or the public. Also how to help parents record memories.

Margaret G. Bigger Vintage Photos Illustrations by Loyd Dillon Paperback
Standard print - 1996 pp. 160 $13.95

You Can Tell You're a Charlottean If...

288 ways that residents (natives, newcomers and long-timers) of Charlotte, North Carolina are different from the rest of the world. Plus Head Scratchers and a Queenz Quiz. 91 locals from all walks of life contributed lines.

Edited by Margaret Bigger & Betsy Webb Cartoons by Loyd Dillon Paperback
LARGE PRINT - 1998 pp. 96 $7.95

See order form - next page.

What's Next?
Churchgoers' Chuckles
You Can Tell You're In Charlotte If...
DaddyHoot - The Lighter Side of Fatherhood
Puppies & All That Waggin'
MotherHoot - The Lighter Side of Motherhood, Vol. II
Kitties & All That Litter, Vol. II.
MEN!/WOMEN!

Order Form

Please complete both sides of this form.

_______ copies of **MEN!**
At the retail price of $7.50 $_____

_______copies of ______________________________

At the retail price of ____________________________ $_____

Plus $2 postage/handling up to 5 books; $4 up to 10 books $_____

NC residents add 6.5% state tax on retail price to:
TOTAL $_____

Autographed? Yes________ No________

Men book to____

Name of recipient's man____

Wedding book to____________________________________
Circle: Bride &/or groom   Mother of the bride   Minister/priest/rabbi

Date of wedding, if known ________________________________

Motherhood book to:___________________________________
Circle: Expectant mom   Mother   Grandmother

Names of children, if known ______________________________

Cat book to:____

Name of cat/cats_______________________________________

Senior humor book to:___________________________________

Recalling memories book to:______________________________

Charlotte book to: _____________________________________

Your name/ address/ phone number:

Mail form & check to: **A. Borough Books, P.O. Box 15391 Charlotte, NC 28211**

Contributor's Form

Here are some great ideas for **MEN!/WOMEN!** - the sequel to **MEN!**, which will give men "equal time" and women a chance to tell us what we missed.

____

____

____

____

____

____

____

____

____

____

____

Please fill out name and address on the back.

Contributor's name____

Address______________________________Phone__________________

City____________________________State/Zip__________________

Comments____

____

____

Please mail this form to:

A. Borough Books
P.O. Box 15391
Charlotte, NC 28211